The Queen's Shadow

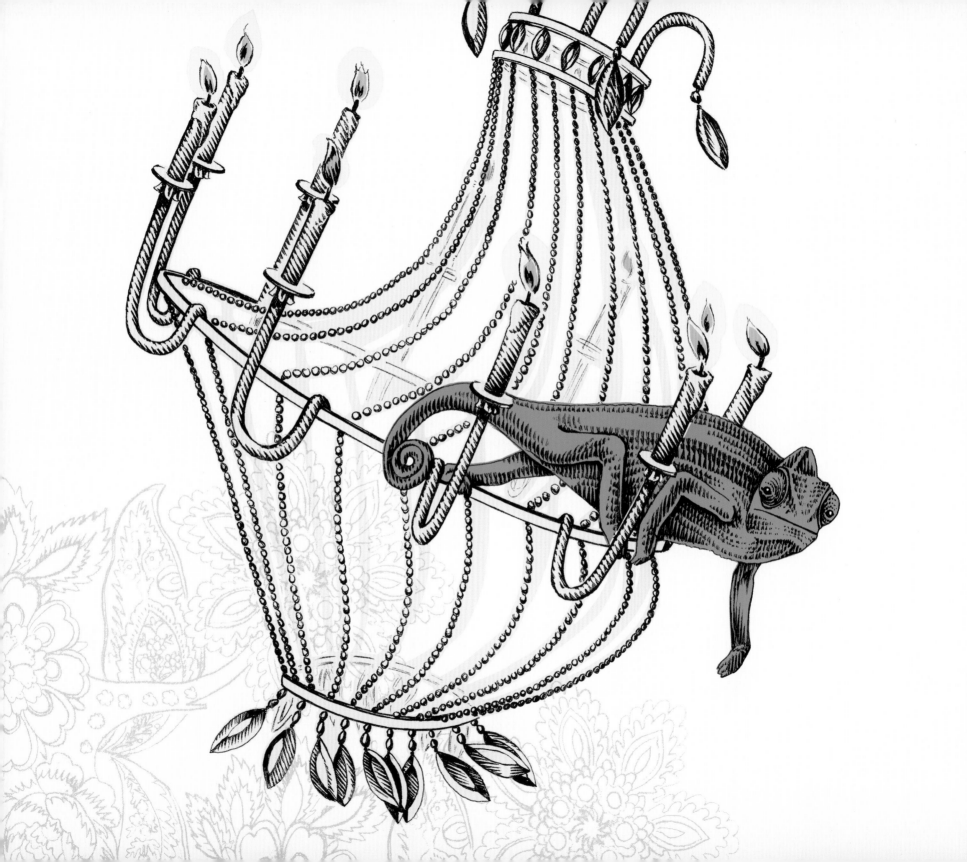

Cybèle Young

THE QUEEN'S SHADOW

A Story About How Animals See

KIDS CAN PRESS

Kids Can Press acknowledges the financial support of
the Government of Ontario, through the Ontario Media
Development Corporation's Ontario Book Initiative;
the Ontario Arts Council; the Canada Council for the Arts;
and the Government of Canada, through the CBF, for our
publishing activity.

Published in Canada by   Published in the U.S. by
Kids Can Press Ltd.   Kids Can Press Ltd.
25 Dockside Drive   2250 Military Road
Toronto, ON M5A 0B5   Tonawanda, NY 14150

www.kidscanpress.com

The artwork in this book was rendered in pen and ink
and colored in Photoshop.
The text is set in Incognito and Celeste.

Acquired by Karen Li
Edited by Stacey Roderick
Designed by Karen Powers

This book is smyth sewn casebound.
Manufactured in Shenzhen, China, in 11/2014 by C & C Offset

CM 15 0 9 8 7 6 5 4 3 2 1

Library and Archives Canada Cataloguing in Publication

Young, Cybèle, 1972–, author, illustrator
    The queen's shadow : a story about how animals see /
Cybèle Young.

Interest age level: Ages 7–11.
ISBN 978-1-894786-60-7 (bound)

    1. Vision — Juvenile literature. I. Title.

QP475.7.Y69 2014   j573.8'8   C2013-908035-X

Kids Can Press is a Corus™ Entertainment company

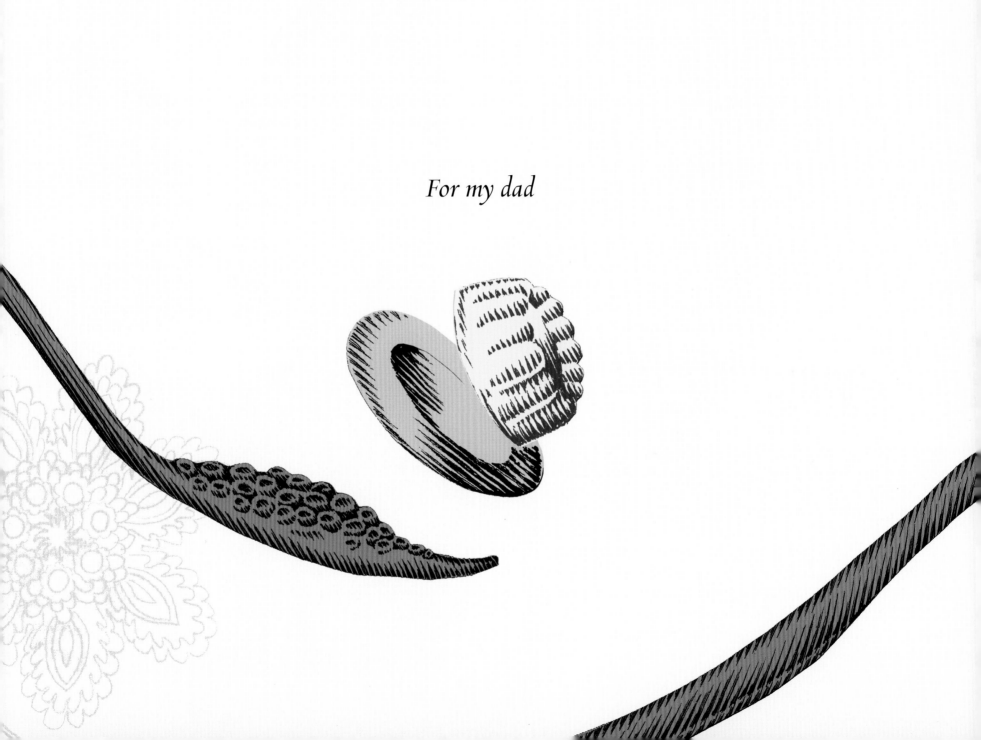

For my dad

$\mathcal{T}$he Queen's Ball had begun like any other of her royal parties — lavish displays of food and festive entertainment were being enjoyed by society's most important nobility.

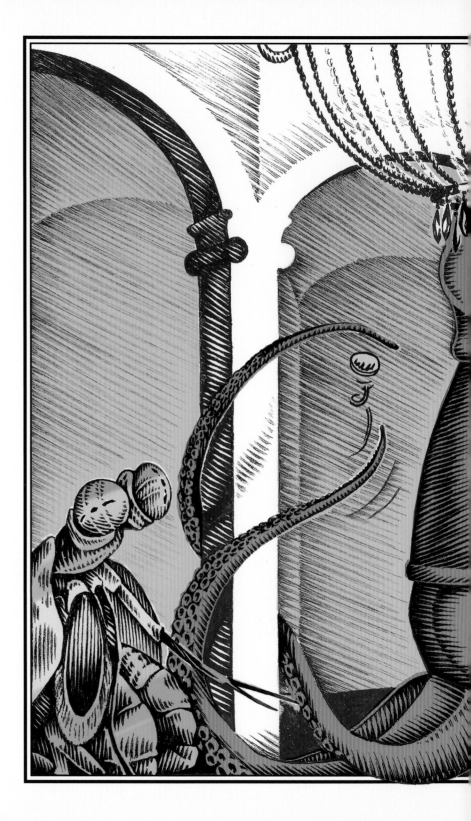

Suddenly, there was a CRASH and a KAPOW as lightning lit up the room.

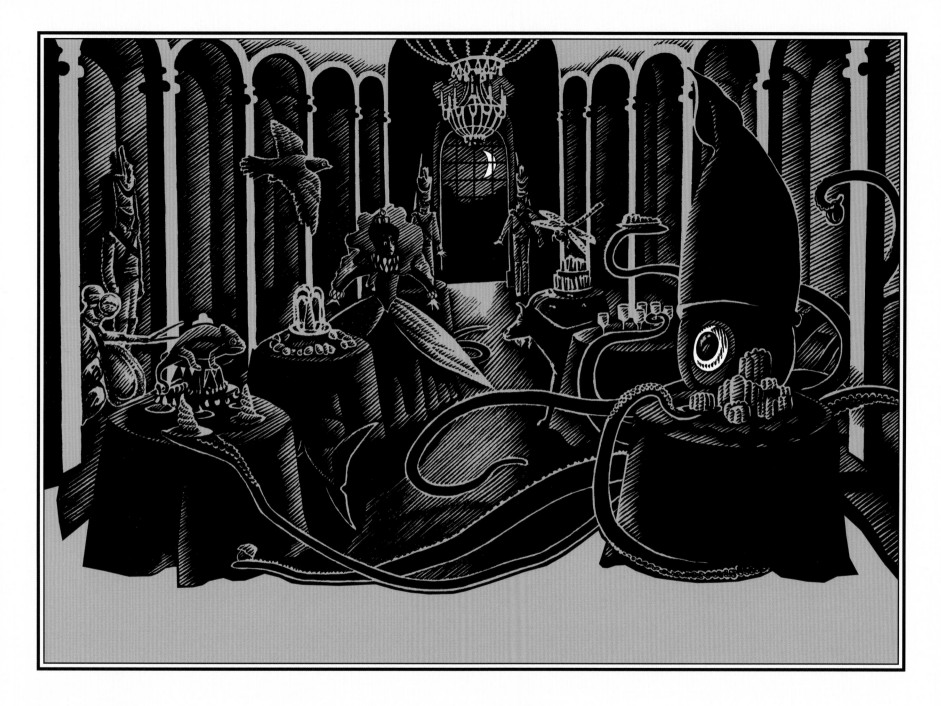

Then all went DARK.

Moments later, the lights returned, giving way to a bloodcurdling

Aaaaaaiieeeee!

"Someone has stolen my shadow!!" screamed the Queen.

Chaos ensued. A major crime had been committed, and it was necessary to enforce order.

"Stay RIGHT where you are — EVERY one of you! Move not a muscle." The unmistakably authoritative words came from none other than Mantis Shrimp, the Royal Detective.

After scanning the room for what seemed like mere seconds, he announced, "AH, YES — I HAVE IT!"

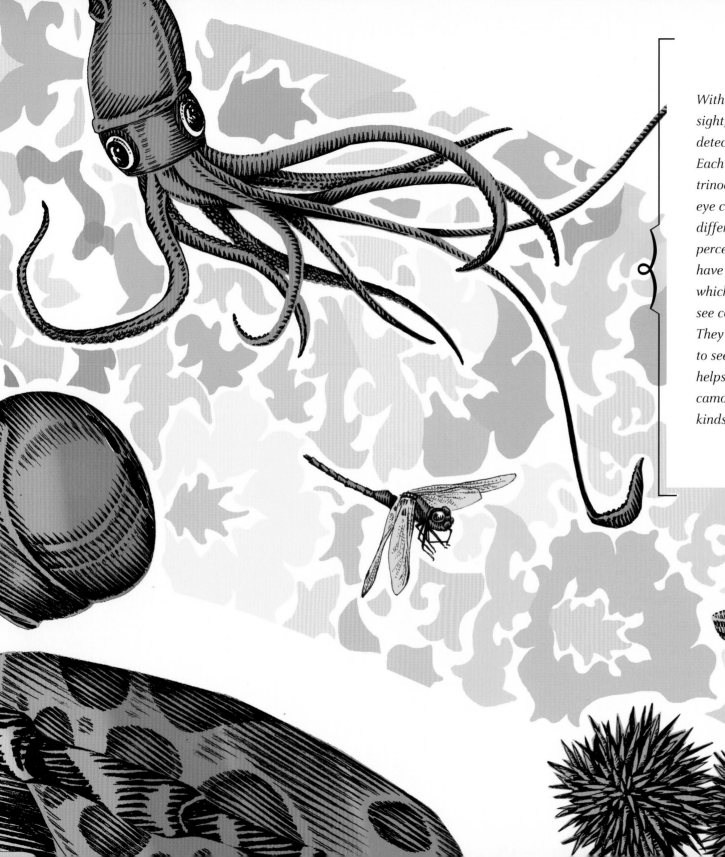

With its extraordinary powers of sight, a **mantis shrimp** can detect a needle in a haystack. Each of its two eyes has trinocular vision, meaning the eye can see objects from three different angles for extra depth perception. Mantis shrimp eyes have 16 photoreceptors, 12 of which are specially adapted to see colors invisible to humans. They also have a superior ability to see polarized light, which helps the mantis shrimp see the camouflaged, almost invisible kinds of fish it likes to eat.

"The one responsible for this crime is ... Sir Chameleon! In typical chameleon fashion, he virtually disappeared by blending in with his surroundings. From there, he projected his tongue, snatched the shadow and swallowed it in one gulp!" Mantis Shrimp was quite satisfied with his deduction.

"APPALLING!" declared the Queen. "How could you, Sir Chameleon?!"

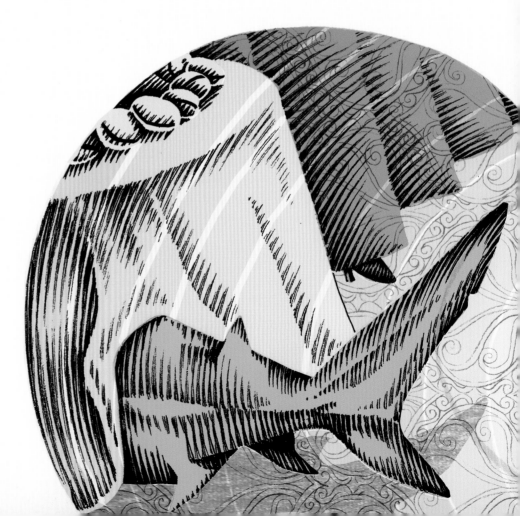

Shocked and trembling, Sir Chameleon stood up for himself. "But that is impossible! I cannot take aim until both of my eyes focus on a single target."

He continued, "Sir *Shrimp*, at the time of the lightning flash, each of my eyes was moving independently as I looked for my next tasty morsel. At that time I noticed both Dragonfly catching a fly *and* the ripple of the pink tablecloth ... under which I'm certain I saw Captain Shark's tail fin disappear ... right at Her Majesty's feet!"

The eyes of a **chameleon** can look in different directions at the same time. But when using its eyes independently, chameleons have no depth perception. Only once both eyes are focused on the same thing can they see in three dimensions to aim and shoot out their tongue in order to catch their next meal.

The Queen and the rest of the room GASPED in disbelief.

"I will remind you, and everyone else for that matter, that
I most certainly am NOT a *shrimp*!" huffed the Royal Detective.
He then continued: "However, I believe you could be onto something.
Captain Shark, can you defend yourself against these accusations?"

"I most certainly can." All eyes now rested on the captain, whose
command of the room was admirable.

"It is true I was under the banquet table — I'll take your word for the color
of its cloth — but I was simply going after a fallen cod cake. And as you'll see,
it remains in that spot. I missed the cake because I was distracted by the sight
of Lancehead coiled right there on the floor. She had the rest of you fooled
into thinking she was part of the carpet pattern!"

Because Captain Shark was a respected member of society,
with what sounded like a believable story, the suspected snake
was swiftly seized by the Royal Guards.

Although it is likely that **sharks** cannot see color, they have a superior ability to perceive contrast. A layer of mirrored crystals behind the part of the eye called the retina increases the amount of light that is detected by the shark's eye. This allows them to see patterns of light and dark, even in murky waters.

"SNEAKY, SLIPPERY SERPENT!" cried the Queen.

Stupefied, Lancehead declared: "I was behind the Queen. I thought it a *sssafe* place to hide from Goat'*sss* trampling feet! (Some proper dance lessons*sss* would do him well.) Goat was coming from Her Majes*ssty's ssside*, and I saw him drawing nearer in the blackout. He was looking straight at Her Maje*sssty.*"

The Royal Guards thought it best to take this highly venomous snake at her word, and Mantis Shrimp couldn't imagine where she could have hidden the shadow. Concluding she was telling the truth, he announced, "It would seem, then, that this crime was committed by Goat, the malodorous Earl of Pancake."

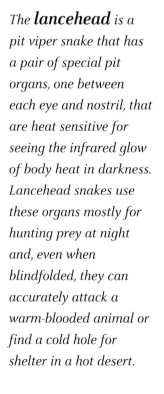

The **lancehead** is a pit viper snake that has a pair of special pit organs, one between each eye and nostril, that are heat sensitive for seeing the infrared glow of body heat in darkness. Lancehead snakes use these organs mostly for hunting prey at night and, even when blindfolded, they can accurately attack a warm-blooded animal or find a cold hole for shelter in a hot desert.

"CUD-CHEWING CRIMINAL!"
cried the Queen.

Goat, nervous and trembling, stumbled
into plain view. "I-I-I didn't see Her Majesty
in front of me — that's my blind spot. I was
trampling around because I was distracted
by Dragonfly whizzing close by me at a great
speed! So close and so quickly, in fact, that I
think, perhaps, she could have been the only
one capable of the crime!"

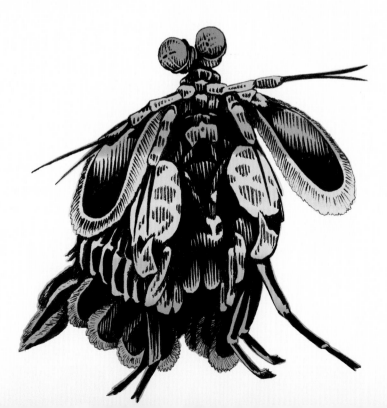

*With their wide, rectangular pupils, **goats** have excellent peripheral vision, like what you might see looking through a panoramic camera lens. As prey animals, they need to see if a predator is approaching. But because their eyes are far apart, they have a blind spot directly in front of them, as well as behind.*

"AWFUL ARTHROPOD!" A distaste for insects made the Queen quick with her blame.

Before the detective had a chance to question the winged speedster, Dragonfly interrupted, "Goat is the object of my affection simply because there is no shortage of flies around him. A good meal is so effortless there that I was able to observe the rest of the party easily while I dined. But I can say with all certainty that, throughout the evening, I have seen Colossal Squid's arms sneakily stretching to virtually every corner of the room tonight."

Mantis Shrimp was losing patience. Were Dragonfly not such a skilled flier, ducking and darting around, she would have been swatted for speaking out of turn. But as she was rather small to carry out a theft of that size, the Royal Dectective turned his attention to the sound of clattering fine china.

Dragonflies are extremely agile fliers, moving quickly and easily. They have compound eyes covering most of their head like a helmet. In a well-lit area, they can see movement in almost all directions at once. Sight is by far their most important sense, used to catch and eat up to 600 insects per day, and to avoid birds, their predators.

"Your Majesty," suggested Mantis Shrimp, "it would seem this freeloading floater IS rather far-reaching."

"MALICIOUS MOLLUSK!" huffed the Queen.

Colossal Squid quickly began, "I'd say you caught me red-handed, only my hands are clearly full! Just ask Captain Shark, who bet me I couldn't collect refreshments from all the tables at once.

"You are aware that I have the largest eyes in the animal kingdom — the size of the very plates I'm balancing. So large are they that I can see great distances in darkness. In the blackout, from across the room, I spotted Dr. Pigeon flapping away in haste, high above the Queen."

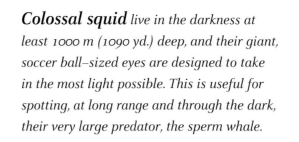

Colossal squid *live in the darkness at least 1000 m (1090 yd.) deep, and their giant, soccer ball–sized eyes are designed to take in the most light possible. This is useful for spotting, at long range and through the dark, their very large predator, the sperm whale.*

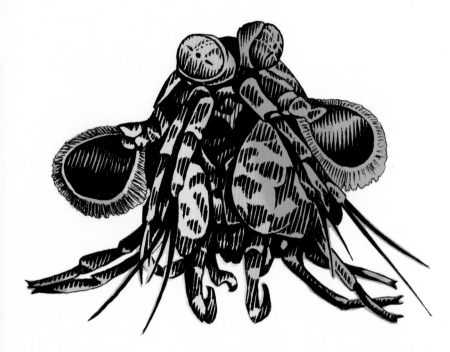

The Royal Detective, now exhausted by the length of
his investigation, simply gestured at the feathered professor
of math to explain himself.

"I flew in haste — yes — to gain higher ground where I am safe
from predators. This is something I always do when darkness falls,
as I cannot see at night," said Dr. Pigeon.

"Normally I'm too busy calculating important information to look
for shadows, but I do enjoy the challenge of a puzzle.

"If I put my attention to the floor, the most logical area to focus on,
I can recall that at precisely 7:42 p.m., 7:56 p.m., 8:04 p.m. and, most
interestingly, at the flash before the blackout at 8:11 p.m., I saw movement
in the shadowy areas. And now, at 8:37 p.m. ... I see it again!

"Romanoff! Echino! Show yourselves!"

As well as having great powers of concentration and observation, **pigeons** have extraordinary eyesight. They can see movement from great distances and many more colors than humans will ever know, well into the range of ultraviolet. Humans have long been aware of this, having used pigeons as messengers for thousands of years and, more recently, in search-and-rescue missions.

The two young sea urchins skittered out from under a table. Mantis Shrimp leaned down and spoke softly and slowly. "Children, what do you know about the whereabouts of the Queen's shadow?"

"We've been playing hide-and-seek in everyone's shadows all night. But we've avoided the Queen since her return from the ladies' room over an hour ago — as she has had no shadow to hide in ever since!"

They were giggling so hard, they could barely carry on.

"She left her shadow in ...

THE LOO!"

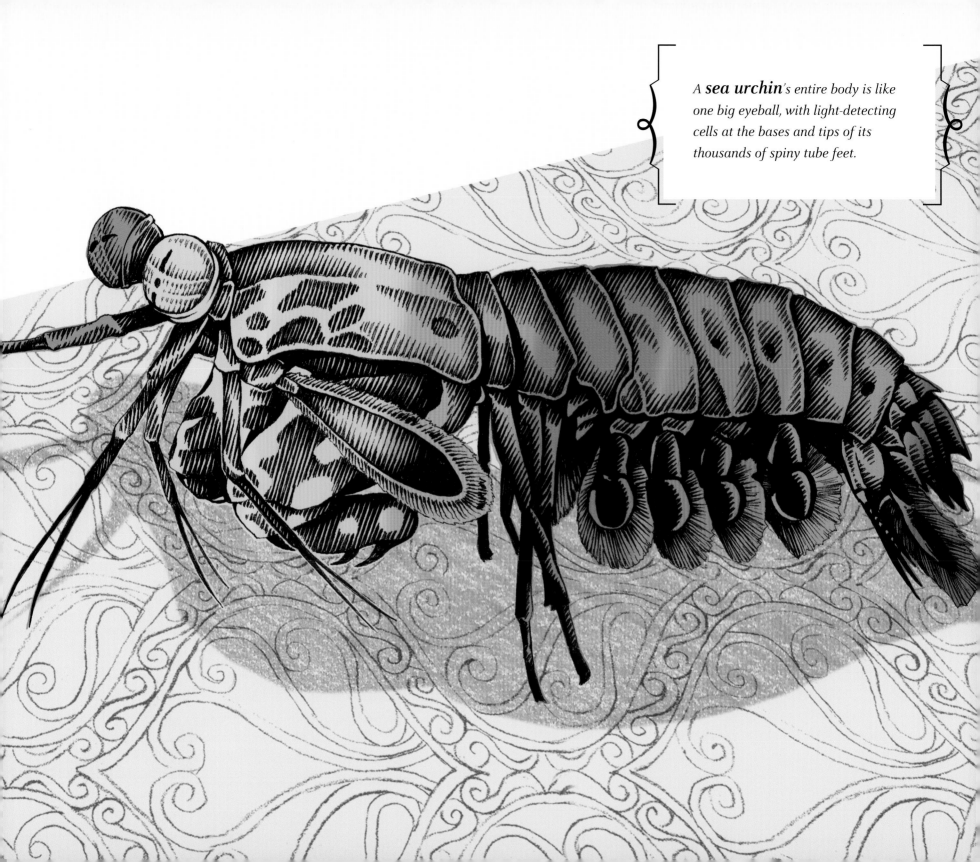

A **sea urchin**'s entire body is like one big eyeball, with light-detecting cells at the bases and tips of its thousands of spiny tube feet.

Everyone in the room was shocked into an embarrassed silence.

The Queen turned pink, then crimson, and then finally a hue perceptible only by those creatures able to see a wider spectrum of color than humans.

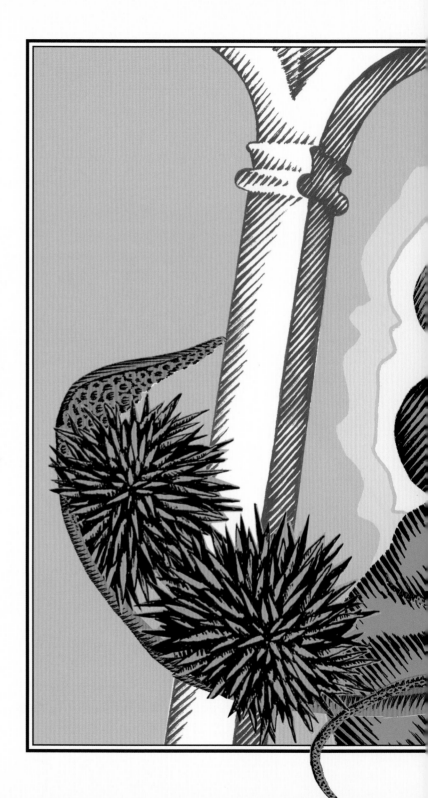

The Royal Guards quickly obtained the misplaced shadow from the powder room. The Queen, struck speechless, was then escorted back to her private quarters. The Royal Detective diverted the crowd's attention with a few parting words: "I will take this opportunity to impress upon you that, with so many points of view in this room tonight, I trust in your ability to see this situation clearly for what it is — a mysterious crime solved by my thorough investigation — the details about which not a word shall be spoken, for the sake of Her Majesty's dignity."

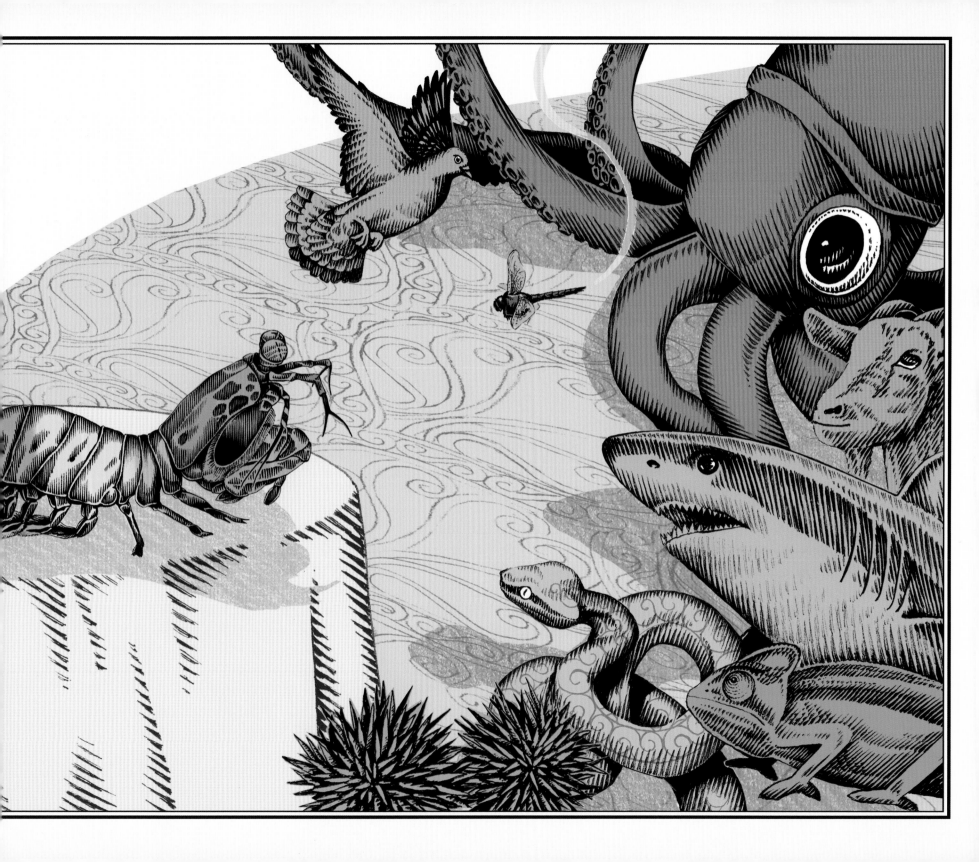

The guests were ushered out, deep in thought. It wasn't until they were past the palace gates that they realized they had each left something behind.

But all was not lost. While they may now be minus the darkness
of their shadows, they have gained the light of new perspectives.

What is vision?

The information about vision included in this story is based on scientific research, but we can really only guess how the different animals actually see. We do know for sure how humans see, though.

Follow the path of light from the image of the Queen into your brain, and you'll understand how amazing the process of vision is.

❶ THE CORNEA

The strong outer layer of your eye has one clear and protective "window" called the cornea. It curves out to gather and focus light from a wide field of view.

❷ THE IRIS AND PUPIL

In order to let in just the right amount of light for your eyes to see things comfortably, rings of tiny muscles inside your eyes control the iris to make your pupils bigger or smaller. When we talk about eye color, we mean the color of the iris. The pupil has no color because it is a hole or gap surrounded by the edges of the iris.

❸ THE LENS

This is a perfectly clear and very flexible part of your eye. Its shape is made rounder or flatter by another ring of muscles inside the eye. This is how you focus on objects close up or farther away. Your cornea and lens work their magic together by bending the light to form a small, sharp image on the retina. The lens makes the image upside down and backward (see, for example, the Queen's image).

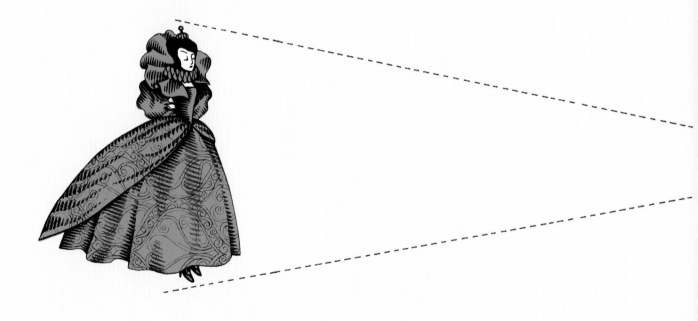

❺ THE RETINA

The retina is a thin layer of light-sensitive nerve cells (photoreceptors) that connect directly to your brain. There are two main kinds of nerve cells that make up your retina: about 100 million called rods and another 7 million called cones.

❹ THE HUMORS

There are two clear, jelly-like substances in the eye called the aqueous (watery) and vitreous (glassy) humors. They hold the shape of the eye and protect all the parts inside it. They also help nourish the clear parts of the eye — the lens and cornea — which have no blood supply.

Rods are about a hundred times more sensitive to light than cones, but it is your cones that see color. When light hits these cells, they convert its energy into the chemical and electrical signals that are the "language" your brain understands as different colors.

6 THE OPTIC NERVE

All the information from the retinas travels directly to your brain through the "superhighway" of connections in your optic nerves. The nerve pathway from each eye crosses over and feeds into the opposite side of your brain: left eye to right brain, right eye to left brain. In fact, the right side of your brain controls the left side of your body and vice versa.

7 THE BRAIN

Without your brain none of this information would make any sense at all. Vision — the processing part of it — really happens in the visual cortex, by far the largest part of your brain. This is where that image of the Queen, which appears upside down and backward on the retina, is understood the right way around. And that's only a small part of all the work our brains perform to make sense of what we see. Size, distance, color, meaning and countless other amazing judgments are made by our brains and stored in our memories. Most incredible of all, this happens almost instantly and constantly every waking minute of every day.

More about the animals in this book

MANTIS SHRIMP

The mantis shrimp is not actually a shrimp at all but gets its name because it looks like a cross between a praying mantis and a shrimp. A truly impressive creature, this marine crustacean can grow up to about 30 cm (12 in.) in length and sometimes longer. Mantis shrimp live among coral reefs in tropical and semitropical seas. They can be divided into two groups based on their behavior: the spearers and the smashers. Spearers use their specially adapted limb to stab and slash their prey. A smasher's "punch" is so powerful that it can break the glass of an aquarium with a single blow.

CHAMELEON

The chameleon's tongue is just about as amazing as its eyes. It can extend from one to two times the length of its body (not including the tail), and it shoots out three times faster than a blink of your eye — about $\frac{1}{15}$ of a second. As well, the end of the tongue isn't just sticky, it also traps the insect with suction and special scaly cells. Chameleons change color in response to temperature, light intensity and mood. This is more to do with communication than camouflage, but they are often hard to see as their color range matches that of their typical habitats.

SHARK

Sharks have lived in our seas for over 400 million years. Although their skeletons are made of cartilage (like the hard but flexible parts of your ear), their jaws are strengthened by a layer of tiny crystal plates called tesserae (or tiles), making them powerful and effective biters. Sharks that feed on larger prey like seals and tuna have some rows of teeth with sharp points that are good for grabbing and others with serrated edges good for cutting. They shed their teeth almost as easily as a cat sheds its fur. Some species go through up to 30 000 teeth in their lifetimes.

LANCEHEAD PIT VIPER SNAKE

Pit vipers are venomous snakes found all around the world in temperate to tropical climates. They help the environment by keeping the population of mice and other rodents in balance, but they also eat birds, lizards and other snakes. Most pit vipers, like rattlesnakes, are shy around humans and attack only when threatened. Their venom is a form of digestive juice, like saliva. Surprisingly, many of the very ingredients in venom that disable or kill a snake's prey have been found to be useful in treating some human health problems, such as high blood pressure, strokes and even some kinds of cancer.

GOAT

Although most people think goats will eat anything, including cardboard and tin cans, they can be picky eaters. They will avoid spoiled food unless they are really hungry. On the other hand, goats are very curious and do eat a wide variety of plants. It is more likely a goat will nibble the cardboard or "taste" a tin can because of what it contains and not because they want to eat it. Goats are known to be a runner-up to dogs as "man's best friend," but they are very independent animals and will easily return to the wild if given the chance.

DRAGONFLY

Predatory dragonflies the size of modern seagulls ruled the air 300 million years ago. Now there are almost 6000 much smaller species of dragonflies known in the world. All are excellent fliers and do just about everything in the air except rest. Dragonflies have two pairs of sturdy, flexible wings, which they can control separately or together. In addition to hovering and gliding, they can move in the air in six directions: upward, downward, forward, backward, left and right. They are expert hunters, feeding on other insects. They especially love mosquitoes and can eat up to 100 a day.

COLOSSAL SQUID

Little is known of the colossal squid since it has never been observed in its natural habitat, up to 2 km (1¼ mi.) below the surface of the Southern Ocean that circles the globe around Antarctica. Some information has been learned from captured specimens. The colossal squid is believed to be the largest invertebrate (animal without a skeleton), possibly growing up to 14 m (45 ft.) long — as tall as a four-story house. Its mouth is like an upside-down parrot's beak, used to chop up prey into small chunks. This is necessary because the colossal squid's throat passes through the middle of its donut-shaped brain before reaching the stomach.

PIGEON

Pigeons are much smarter than most people give them credit for. They can tell direction by detecting the earth's magnetic field. They have a great sense of smell and can remember scents from the different areas they fly through. Pigeons can remember hundreds of different images for years. It also appears that they have a good memory for landmarks and can even follow roads as a guide. Scientists have even shown that pigeons can learn to tell the difference between paintings created by artists like Picasso and Monet.

SEA URCHIN

Sea urchins are found worldwide along the rocky ocean floor, most commonly in coral reefs. They move around by pumping water in and out of their rows of tube feet. Sea urchins are omnivorous and eat almost anything they come across. They are also eaten by a wide range of creatures. Although they aren't aggressive, many species of sea urchins have two defense mechanisms: venom-filled spines and tiny, claw-like structures down between their spines that can inject a painful poison. As an additional form of defense, sea urchins use their tube feet to cover themselves with objects and hide under rocks.

Glossary

Arthropod: Arthropods are animals that have exoskeletons (outer, armor-like skeletons), jointed limbs and segmented bodies. They do *not* have backbones. Dragonflies, spiders and shrimp are just a few examples of arthropods.

Color: Each color is created by a specific wavelength of light energy. When we see a color, it is because that wavelength is what is being reflected, or bounced back, for our eyes to see. The other color wavelengths have been absorbed by the object, so we don't see them. For example, a lemon looks yellow because the skin of the lemon reflects only yellow light.

Compound eye: Compound eyes are made up of hundreds or even thousands of little tube-like eyes that work together. Each of these tubes, called ommatidia (meaning "little eyes"), has a tiny lens made by the cornea at one end and photoreceptors at the other. All these little eyes working together gives an insect a very wide view and is excellent for seeing small, quick movements of prey (like mosquitoes) or predators (like humans with flyswatters).

Depth perception: The ability to see the world in three dimensions (3D) — that is, see that things have height, width and length — is called depth perception.

Infrared: Infrared is a kind of light energy that is invisible to human eyes, but can be detected by special heat sensors in some animals, such as pit vipers. All warm bodies and objects give off infrared energy, which is why these snakes have no trouble hunting for mice or rabbits in their dark burrows.

Loo: The "loo" is another word for "restroom" or "toilet." It comes from the French word *l'eau*, meaning water. Other words for this useful place are "bathroom," "washroom," etc.

Mollusk: Mollusks are a diverse family of creatures, many of which live in seas and oceans, rivers and lakes. Snails and slugs are mollusks that live on land, but are still relatives of sea creatures such as the colossal squid and the octopus.

Photoreceptor: Photoreceptors are the special cells in eyes that change light energy into the electrical and chemical energy that a nervous system and brain use to create a picture of the world.

Polarized Light: Polarized light is not easily detected by the human eye — we most often see it as glare. Normally light waves vibrate in all directions. But when light waves reflect off a shiny surface, such as fish scales or a glass window, they are flattened into one direction of vibration, or polarized.

Predator: A predator is a creature that hunts other animals for food.

Prey: A prey animal is a creature that is hunted and eaten by other animals.

Spectrum: A spectrum is a range of colors, such as the visible colors that make up a rainbow. Visible light, however, is just a small part of a much wider spectrum of energy. If you could see the infrared light in a rainbow, it would be next to the outer band of red; ultraviolet light would be next to the inner band of violet.

Tube feet: Creatures like sea urchins and starfish move around using tube feet. The feet act like little suction cups, grabbing and releasing the surface they are on to move the creature around.

Ultraviolet light: Ultraviolet (UV) light is invisible to human eyes, but visible to the photoreceptors of many insects, as well as some birds and other creatures.